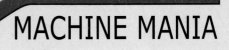

MACHINE MANIA

EXTREME
BOATS

Frances Ridley

ticktock

Copyright © ticktock Entertainment Ltd 2007
First published in Great Britain in 2007 by ticktock Media Ltd.,
Unit 2, Orchard Business Centre, North Farm Road,
Tunbridge Wells, Kent, TN2 3XF

ticktock project editor: Julia Adams
ticktock project designer: Emma Randall

We would like to thank: Alix Wood.

ISBN 978 1 84696 565 4

Printed in China
9 8 7 6 5 4 3 2

Picture credits:
b=bottom; c=centre; t=top; r=right; l=left
Alamy: 19t, 25t; Bethen of Cowes: 16-17; British Antarctic Survey: 12-13; Corbis: 2, 8-9c,
14-15, 17t, 18-19; Hawkes Ocean Technologies: 9t; John Clark Photography: 3, 4-5c;
RNLI: 20-21; Stena: 22-23; ticktock Picture Archive: 5t, 6-7, back cover cl;
World of Residence: 10-11, back cover cr; Yamaha: 23t.

Every effort has been made to trace the copyright holders,
and we apologise in advance for any unintentional omissions.
We would be pleased to insert the appropriate acknowledgements
in any subsequent edition of this publication.

Contents

California Quake Drag Boat

Drag boats are the fastest racing boats. They are more like rockets than boats. The California Quake can go at 370 km/h.

The top of the Quake breaks free if there is a crash. This helps to keep the driver safe.

The driver's helmet is linked to a bottle of air. They can breathe underwater if they have to.

Polaris Virage TX Jetski

Jetski riders surf across the waves at high speed. A jetski can go at nearly 97 km/h! You **steer** it with handlebars – just like a bike.

Jetski riders can
do turns, jumps
and loops.
They can even
dive underwater!

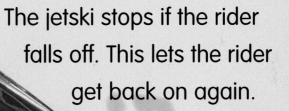

The jetski stops if the rider
falls off. This lets the rider
get back on again.

Deep Flight Submersible

A submersible is a boat that can go underwater. The Deep Flight is small – it only holds one person. It is used to explore the deep sea.

The Deep Flight has four cameras. It has six lights because it's totally dark in the deep sea.

The Deep Flight has a pair of short wings. These pull the submersible down through the water.

The World Luxury Liner

The passengers on The World aren't on holiday – they live there! They buy a set of rooms and then travel all over the planet.

The World's **hull** is made of huge pieces of **steel**. The pieces were put together by giant cranes.

The World has 12 **decks**. Each deck has lots of things to do. There are restaurants, clubs, theatres, swimming pools and cinemas!

James Clark Ross Research Ship

Research ships take scientists to explore different places. They can spend months at sea. The scientists live on the ship.

The James Clark Ross can smash through thick ice. It weighs 5,732 tonnes – that's more than 30 jumbo jets put together! Its **hull** is made of strong **steel**.

The James Clark Ross is in **Antarctica**. 31 scientists work on the ship. They find out about the sea and the weather.

Los Angeles Fireboats

Los Angeles is in America. It has a big **port** and six fireboats. Fireboats fight fires on ships and buildings by the sea.

Each
boat has
six powerful pumps.
They suck in water and
fire it out of water-guns.
The guns shoot jets of
water as high as
150 metres.

Nimitz-Class Aircraft Carrier

The Nimitz-class aircraft carrier is a huge warship. It is as long as three football pitches.

The Nimitz carries 85 planes and 6 helicopters. Fuel for the planes and helicopters is kept in tanks. These tanks are the size of swimming pools!

It uses the latest computers and **radar**.

The Nimitz has over 6,000 crew members. They eat 20,000 meals a day!

Jahre Viking Oil Supertanker

Oil supertankers are the biggest ships in the world. The Jahre Viking's deck is as large as four football pitches.

The ship is so big that the crew use bikes to get around!

18

The Jahre Viking takes the oil to a **refinery**. It travels very slowly – its top speed is only 18 km/h.

Trent-Type Lifeboat

Lifeboats rescue people from the sea. They are strong boats with brave crews!

The Trent-Type Lifeboat has a top speed of 46 km/h. It can carry 6 crew and 10 survivors.

20

The crew use **radar** and radio to **track** ships that are in trouble.

Rescued people go to the survivors' **cabin**. The cabin has heaters, clothes, hot drinks and snacks.

Lifeboat

Catamaran Car Ferries

Ferries carry passengers, cars and goods. Catamaran ferries have two **hulls** instead of one. The hulls cut through the waves. This makes the ride smoother and faster.

The Stena Discovery has four huge engines. They are as powerful as 600 car engines!

This catamaran holds 200 cars and 1,000 passengers. It also has bars and restaurants on board.

Glossary

Antarctica   An area of the world that is covered in ice and snow.

Cabin   A room on a ship.

Deck   The floor of a ship.

Hull   Main part of a ship – the part that floats on the water.

Port   Place where ships can stay between trips.

Radar   Way of spotting objects that are far away.

Refinery   Place where oil is turned into petrol.

Research   Finding out about some something.

Steel   Very strong metal.

Steer   To control the movement or direction of something.

Track   To follow something.